The

Noble Woman

Aliya Butt

Ta-Ha Publishers
1 Wynne Road
London SW9 0BB
UK

Copyright © Ta-Ha Publishers Ltd.

Published Sha'ban 1421/November 2000
2nd Edition 2004
by
Ta-Ha Publishers Ltd.
1 Wynne Road
London SW9 0BB
website: www.taha.co.uk
email: sales@taha.co.uk

By: Aliya Butt
General Editor: Dr. Abia Afsar-Siddiqui
Edited by: Abdassamad Clarke

British Library Cataloguing in Publication Data
The Noble Woman
1. Butt, Aliya

ISBN 1 84200 020 9

Typeset by: Bookwright
Web site: www.bogvaerker.dk/Bookwright
Email: bookwright@bogvaerker.dk
Printed & bound by: De-Luxe Printers
                  London NW10 7NR

CONTENTS

"The whole world is a provision,

and the best object of benefit in the world

is a right-acting woman."

(Sahih Muslim)

ACKNOWLEDGEMENTS

This short book would not have been
accomplished without Allah's kind blessings
and the inspiration from my parents & family.
Thanks to my father for his help on Islamic concepts.

Thank you to my cousin Mohammed Zishan Sheikh
for offering his computer skills but most of all
to my brother Mohammed Irfan Butt
without whose support I would never
have reached the end of this book.
May Allah reward you all and reward
those who taught me all I know.

INTRODUCTION

In no other deen or culture are women regarded with such dignity and high esteem as in Islam. Yet even in the new millennium, misconceptions are held by non-Muslims and by some Muslims, who believe that Islam is oppressive in its treatment of women and that the Western woman is far more liberated than her Muslim counterpart. These misconceptions are the result of ignorance. If only people cared to follow the teachings of Allah and His Messenger and His revelations, they would see how Islam emancipated woman from male subjection and granted her a wide array of rights which no other religion or culture had ever provided for its womenfolk.

History reminds us of how the Christians and Jews considered woman a curse, because, in their view, she enticed Adam and brought about his fall from the Garden. An ecclesiastic described woman as 'a foe to friendship, an escapable punishment, a necessary evil'.

In ancient India, a woman was treated like a 'bondmaid' (a captive slave). The Romans considered women to be no more valuable than any of their other personal belongings.

At the beginning of the nineteenth century, in English law, women too had virtually no rights. They were the chattels of their fathers and husbands. They were bought and sold in marriage. They could not vote; they could not sign contracts.

When married, they could not own property. They had no rights over their children and no control over their bodies.

Their husbands could rape and beat them without legal reprisals.

Only by the late nineteenth century did the situation begin to improve in English law. Women in the US waited as late as the twentieth century before the Universal Declaration on Human Rights (1945) finally put women on a par with men and stated that:

"All human beings are born free and equal in dignity and rights".

However, Islam took the hand of woman and honoured her with greater freedom and rights co-equal to man, (except where her own nature dictated otherwise) fourteen centuries before the thought of equality had occurred to any British or US legislator.

The Glorious Qur'an is living proof of Islam's resolution of the inequities between man and woman. To begin with, in the Qur'an Allah corrects the early belief held by the Christians and Jews regarding the 'fall of Adam' for which they blamed Hawwa alone. Allah clarifies that Adam and Hawwa, peace be upon both of them, were equally to blame and shaytan misled both. However, both turned to Allah in repentance and both were forgiven. In one *ayah*, Adam ﷺ was specifically blamed (Surah 20: 121).

Furthermore, Islam waged war on the heinous crime of female infanticide, which was common in many parts of Arabia before the advent of Islam (Surah 16: 58-59). Allah also gave women rights of 'inheritance' (Surah 4: 7), which had been previously denied, and the Prophet ﷺ declared that they could not be forced into marriages (Ibn Majah 1873). In fact, woman is so highly valued, that it is mentioned that the Garden is at the feet of the mother (Ibn Majah, Ibn Hanbal). Yet today, the West, (having forgotten their own histories and struggles for equality), are quick to select Islamic Laws, such as the concept of *hijab* (modesty) and polygamy and criticise them without any background knowledge. Falsities are further caused to permeate via shaytan's best device, the media, thwarting the truth and leaving Islam accused of being oppressive.

We constantly hear stories about violent and exploitative Muslim men, who restrict their women to the home, deprive them of education and career, and force them into marriages. More recently, the outcry surrounding female genital mutilation in Africa has sent shockwaves around the world. The reality is that these practices form part of a 'culture', not part of Islam.

Islam is not a religion of terror and was not spread throughout the world with the 'sword' as perceived by the West. Rather, it is a thoughtful, peaceful and modest religion, which brings us all closer to our Lord.

Unfortunately today we live in an environment devoured by non-Muslims who are accustomed to partying, clubbing, drinking, romancing, free mixing and the like.

One only has to look around today to witness the signs of Judgement Day drawing near. We are living in a largely immoral world where vanity dominates, crime accelerates, sexual anarchy proliferates yet tragically, honour seems to stagnate.

It is high time therefore, that we stopped wasting time indulging in worldly pleasures. Our brief life on this earth is a probation and we must endeavour to achieve the real success and bliss of the Garden. It is therefore important for all Muslims to seek knowledge from the Noble Qur'an and the teachings of the noble Prophet Muhammad ﷺ to ensure that we can distinguish between right and wrong and safely dispel some of the common myths that people hold.

Abiding by laws and rules is not a new concept. Today, we live in a law-abiding society where we follow laws laid down by Governments. The laws are condensed into volumes of legislation and case law helps us understand the application of the rules. This is how social order is maintained.

It follows then that if man has the sense to create laws to maintain social order, surely there must be laws to help maintain man?

By simple analogy, our Creator, Allah, exalted is He, sent down a law book in the form of the Noble Qur'an, not to maintain order in only one society, but to guide and instruct the whole of humanity. Just as the Qur'an has recorded the punishment for those who stray from the path of right action so too does it emphasise the reward for those who do not.

Amongst the 114 surahs (chapters) in the Glorious Qur'an, are those relating to the status of women, surahs an-Nisa (The Women), al-Ahzab (The Confederates), and an-Nur (The Light) being the most prevalent. It is the latter of these surahs in which the overall Islamic behaviour required for women is explained and will be explored in this book.

Joining the crew of shaytan will open the gateway to the Fire, but the key to the Garden is dependent upon good deeds, obedience to Allah and upon every sister striving to become a 'noble woman'.

Background to the Commands on Correct Islamic Behaviour

If the aim for all women is to become 'noble' then the starting point is to understand what nobility means. One would link the word to moral excellence, chastity, and honour. It follows then, that for a Muslim woman to achieve the highest and most valued status of all, it is incumbent upon her to observe correct Islamic behaviour.

The main commands on this are fivefold and are outlined in the following Qur'anic ayat 30 and 31 of Surat an-Nur:

Say to the muminun that they should lower their eyes
    and guard their private parts.
        That is purer for them.
    Allah is aware of what they do.
Say to the mumin women that they should lower their eyes
    and guard their private parts
        and not display their adornments -
            except for what normally shows -
        and draw their head-coverings across
            their breasts.
They should only display their adornments to their husbands
    or their fathers or their husbands' fathers,
    or their sons or their husbands' sons
    or their brothers or their brothers' sons
    or their sisters' sons
    or other women
    or those they own as slaves
    or their male attendants who have no sexual desire

or children who still have no awareness
of women's private parts.
Nor should they stamp their feet
so that their hidden ornaments are known.
Turn to Allah every one of you, muminun,
so that hopefully you will have success.

The above can be summarised as follows:

1. Lowering the eyes
2. Not displaying their beauty and ornaments except what must ordinarily appear thereof
3. Drawing their veils over their bosoms
4. Rules on who can be a woman's *mahram*
5. Not to strike your feet in order to draw attention.

It is necessary at this stage to briefly highlight the circumstances existing at the time of the revelation of Surat an-Nur to help us understand why the utmost decorum had to and has to be observed at all times.

After the successful Battle of Badr, the Muslims began to gain strength. When the *kuffar* realised that they could not defeat Islam on the battlefield, they chose the 'moral' front to carry on the conflict. Their malicious designs led them to start a campaign of lies against the Prophet ﷺ and his followers in order to destroy their superiority. The chief of the hypocrites, 'Abdullah bin Ubayy, made one such vindictive attack on the honour of the Prophet's youngest and most loved wife, Aisha ﷻ in the incident known as *ifk*.

As the Prophet ﷺ and his followers were returning to Madinah from an expedition, they decided to halt for the night. On this occasion, Aisha ﷻ had accompanied her husband travelling on a camel, veiled from all others.

During the evening she went outside the camp to ease herself. When she returned, she realised that she had lost her valuable necklace and so went back in search for it. In the meantime, her camel keeper assumed she was still seated upon the 'chaise' as she was so lightweight and he had not noted her absence. The camp was thus ordered to move on. When Aisha ﷺ re-appeared and realised she had been left behind, she wisely decided to remain rather than attempt to catch up. She wrapped herself up and sat down to rest in the hope that someone would come back to fetch her.

Some time later, Safwan whose duty it was to make checks after each site was left, spotted Aisha ﷺ and helped in taking her back to her husband. He put her on his camel and led the camel by the nose string back to the camp. However, though they both were innocent, when they caught up with the others, an opportunity arose for enemies to raise a wicked scandal.

'Abdullah ibn Ubayy cried out, "By Allah, she could not have remained chaste. Look, there comes the wife of your Prophet openly on the camel, led by the person with whom she passed the night." The above incident was used to slander the good name of Aisha ﷺ who because of the slanders was subjected to extreme pain and anguish for a whole month.

By the grace of Allah, Aisha ﷺ was honourably absolved from all blame but the incident resulted in the divine rules of Islamic conduct as set out above to guard the sexes and repair the cracks which had appeared in the unity of the Muslims.

Even today, the environment and the social influences that most frequently wreck our spiritual ideals are permeated with sexuality and, especially, its misuse. This can either be in the form of false charges and scandals – as was in the case with the wife of the Prophet ﷺ – or breaches of personal or domestic privacy. Hence, regulating our conduct according to the Qur'an requires strict application.

Although the laws relate to both men and women, this book is written especially to help Muslim women understand and apply the rules to their daily lives and will help them achieve the most precious status of being 'noble women'.

Turkey: Muslim Woman with child

LOWERING THE EYES

Say to the muminun that they should lower their eyes and guard their private parts. That is purer for them. Allah is aware of what they do. Say to the mumin women that they should lower their eyes and guard their private parts... (Surat an-Nur 24: 30-31)

The 'lowering of the eyes' is the first expression of modesty as described by the Qur'an and is applicable equally to men and women. The simple explanation of this is to turn one's gaze away from the faces of passers-by and, in particular, not to caress the attractive features or figures of members of the opposite sex (*The Lawful & Prohibited in Islam* – Yusuf al-Qaradawi). Is there harm in the odd fleeting glance? you ask yourself.

Surely it is fine so long as we, (as is traditionally said) "look but don't touch"? But those who are true to themselves, will confess, that it only takes several amorous looks to excite passions and provoke unlawful desires. 'Eyeing her up', 'checking him out' are but a few of the colloquial phrases used to describe those early perilous looks. Indeed this can act as a catalyst to potential danger, particularly, dangers to chastity.

For this reason, 'lowering the eyes' is an injunction from Allah, exalted is He, in His Speech, the Qur'an, and as explained by Muhammad ﷺ the Messenger of Allah. The Almighty does not like the Muslim woman to flaunt her attractions, but He wants her to protect her beauty and her sexuality for the partner whom she will marry. However very few people today sit on the bus to school, the train to work or walk the streets applying this very clear commandment. One should be warned that failure to adhere to this simple but often overlooked order does indeed often result in endless hurt and sometimes grave consequences.

Our society would be a far nobler and more harmonious place to live in if it was not diseased with unlawful relationships, abortions, sexually transmitted diseases, and disrepute or at the very least, mental anguish. We only have to turn on our television sets to witness the soaps and chat shows swarming with such scandals which if we took the time out to scrutinise, we would eventually agree that each disgrace has its origins in an unlawful look.

It is not surprising then that the rules on modesty are strict, as it is crystal clear that a brazen stare is at best a breach of refined manners in its simplest form and at worst potential mayhem. Thus, Allah, exalted is He, prohibits each and every step, which leads up to and results in the *haram* – the unlawful.

The only way then, in which a woman can safeguard her honour and dignity is by observing this divine command of 'lowering the eye' so that her 'eye' is not used as a sword by *shaytan*, but rather as a shield against him.

Women should not deceive themselves into thinking that it is a good quality to be able to entice and attract men. Behaving unethically or talking loosely to see whether one can attract, is often the mentality of some women who only realise when it is too late, that being stalked or raped is not such a funny matter after all!

Indeed, no one has ever thought highly of those women who go around trying to inflame sexual feelings in others.

It is right that men should behave respectfully towards women, but women should not behave in such a way so as to make a man yearn for that which he should not have. Compared to women, men are more aggressive and dominant by nature. These characteristics are genetically based; in particular, they result from differences between male and female hormones. Thus, if a thing appeals to a man, he is urged from within to acquire it even if it means being hasty, fickle and indiscriminating. On the other hand, woman's nature is one of placidity and coyness. Therefore, unless her nature is so corrupt, a woman will never be so headstrong and dauntless as to make the first advances towards the male.

In view of this, the Prophet Muhammad ﷺ did not regard a woman's looking at another man to be as harmful as a man's looking at another woman, yet the onus seems to lie with the woman neither to incite a man's natural urges, nor to give in to his whims.

Thus, modesty in this respect is not only to guard the weaker sex, but also to guard the spiritual good of the stronger sex.

It is not difficult to ignore a man's attempt at drawing your attention if you apply the Almighty's orders. Showing firm disinterest in a man's unnecessary compliments, winks, smiles or wolf whistles, will send a clear enough message, that he is dealing with a noble and, above all, true Muslim woman who will not be manipulated at any cost. Rest assured then, that it will not be long before he walks away the loser, leaving you as the ultimate victor in the eyes of Allah.

The following ahadith (traditions traced from the Prophet, may Allah bless him and grant him peace) as set out below stress the importance of 'lowering the eye':

The Prophet Muhammad ﷺ told 'Ali ibn Abi Talib ؓ:

"'Ali, do not let a second look follow the first. The first is allowed to you but not the second." (*Ahmad, Abu Dawud & at-Tirmidhi*)

The Prophet ﷺ considered the first look inadvertent and therefore pardonable, but second looks at a person of the opposite sex, which are hungry and lustful, are *zina* (adultery) of the eyes, as they give gratification in an unlawful way.

It has been narrated that:

"On the Day of Judgement, molten lead will be poured into the eyes of the man who looks at the charms of a woman lustfully." (*Takmilah, Fath al-Qadr*. For further ahadith on lowering the gaze, see al-Bukhari 8: 247 and 8: 248)

Ibn 'Abbas ﷺ narrated, "I have not seen anything resembling *lamam* (minor wrong actions) except what Abu Hurairah ﷺ narrated from the Prophet ﷺ who said:

"Allah has written for Adam's son, his share of adultery, which he inevitably commits. The adultery of the eye is looking (at something at which is wrongful to look), and the adultery of the tongue is to utter (what it is unlawful to utter), and the inner self wishes and longs for (adultery) and the private parts turn that into reality or refrain from submitting to the temptation." (*Sahih al-Bukhari* 8: 260)

So, you may pull the wool over the eyes of those around you but the truth can never be hidden from Allah, exalted is He, for:

"Allah knows what the heart contains." (Surat al-Ma'idah 5: 7)

After reading this section, many of you may be surprised at why so much emphasis is placed on something which seems so trivial. Perhaps your alarm bells are ringing because you know that your own gaze has often wandered. Of course in the society in which we live, it is almost impossible not to look at the opposite sex. If you see a man and in your mind happen to admire his attractive features, it is pardonable, but turning your head again and again to get a better look is encouraging the man and sending messages of interest. Such behaviour is prohibited because it will not be long before you start smiling, chatting, exchange numbers, dating him and maybe crossing all moral boundaries before marriage.

Human beings are not infallible and in order to protect the honour of women who inevitably carry the stigma when something goes wrong, Allah, exalted is He, intends that men and women blot out the first of the evils, by lowering the gaze.

Thus, although human nature makes things which are attractive appeal to the eye, this should not be a passport to immoral behaviour.

One may find the ultimate wisdom on this by remembering the words of the Prophet Muhammad ﷺ when he addressed the nation in his poignant Farewell Address and said:

"Beware of shaytan, for the safety of your deen. He has lost all hope of leading you astray in big things, so beware of following him in small things" (9th of Dhul-Hijjah 10 A.H. in the Uranah Valley at Arafat.)

Young Muslima aged 5

English Muslima

Photo: Peter Saunders

MODESTY IN DRESS

A nd not display their adornments – except for what normally shows… (Surat an-Nur 24: 31)

On account of the differentiation of the sexes in nature and temperament, a greater amount of modesty and privacy is required of women than of men, especially in dress.

Our first task is to understand what constitutes 'adornments'.

In accordance with Islamic Shari'ah, this includes the hair, the bosom, the waist and the general outline of the figure.

Revealing such beauty and ornaments to the non-*mahram*[*] would indeed spark off lustful admiration, and the woman who displays herself in this way is just as guilty as the man who craves for her adornment. 'What normally shows' is said to be the clothes and the face and the palms of the hands.

Today, the vast majority of women face ever-increasing pressure to live up to entrenched ideals of female beauty, i.e. to be tall, slim, curvaceous, and sexy. It is the flamboyant display of one's beauty and ornaments, which often determines this success and this is the very flamboyance, which Allah, exalted is He, prohibits.

For the sake of vanity, some women go beyond normality by going through all kinds of treatments from face-lifts, breast enlargements to liposuction, permanent make-up and tanning, thus interfering with their natural beauty. It is no wonder then that the idea of hiding one's beauty, in a society which places so much emphasis on revealing the same, seems almost alien.

---

[*] A male stranger or relative to whom marriage is not prohibited and therefore before whom the rules of dress may not be relaxed.

An American journalist wrote that:

"No matter how happily a woman may be married, it always pleases her to discover that there is a nice man who wishes that she was not." (H.L. Mencken 1880-1956)

It is this type of vanity that Allah, exalted is He, wants to avoid because, apart from driving a woman towards self-indulgence and potential self-destruction, it can also make her fall victim to many men who are unlikely to ignore a lady who reveals all her curves!

In essence, the clothing worn by a Muslim woman is one of choice, taste and style providing the basic requirements are met. These requirements are twofold:

1. The clothing covers all the body, except for hands and face, and is not too tight.

2. The clothing is not so transparent so as to reveal what is underneath.

1. The clothing covers all the body and is not too tight.
In Surat al-Ahzab the following is commanded:

"O Prophet! Tell your wives and daughters and the women of the muminun to draw their outer garments closely round themselves. This makes it more likely that they will be recognised and not be harmed." (Surat al-Ahzab 33: 59)

The object of the above is not to restrict the liberty of women but to protect them from harm and molestation. The rules on covering the body are slightly relaxed when a woman reaches old age and her sexual attractions have diminished.

The Qur'an says on this:

"As for women who are past child-bearing age and no longer have any hope of getting married, there is nothing wrong in their removing their outer clothes, provided they do not flaunt their adornments;

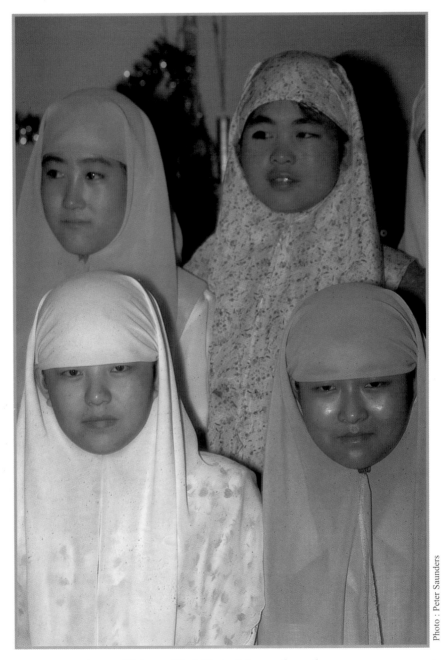

Photo : Peter Saunders

China : Hui Hot girls madrasah.

Photo : Peter Saunders

Sudan : Khartoum University for Women Art Department

but to refrain from doing so is better for them. Allah is All- Hearing, All-Knowing." (Surat an-Nur 24: 58)

In the above sense, some allowances are made for elderly women who have passed their youthful prime. Nevertheless, one must not forget that it is our elders who set precedents for the younger generation and thus modesty is an important virtue to be practised regardless of age.

The following hadith illustrates the importance of avoiding clothes that define the body's curves. On one occasion, Asma, the daughter of Abu Bakr, was visiting her sister Aisha ﷺ the wife of the Prophet ﷺ. When he saw the fabric of Asma's dress, he turned away and said: "If a woman reaches the age of puberty, no part of her body should be seen but this", and he pointed to his face and hands (*Sahih al-Bukhari*). Thus, if clothes are worn that hug the figure, such as body tops, tight trousers and dresses or even tight fitting *shalwar* and *kamees*, or *sari*, then the purpose of the above hadith is defeated, as a woman's adornments would still be clear.

2. The clothing is not so transparent.

It has been narrated that the Prophet ﷺ once received a garment as a gift. He gave it to Usamah ibn Zayd, who in turn gave it to his wife. The Prophet ﷺ then said to Usamah:

> "Ask her to use a *ghulalah** underneath the garment for I fear that it (the garment) may describe the size of her bones." (*Sahih al-Bukhari*)

Abu Hurairah narrated that the Messenger of Allah said that:

> "[of] the types of the denizens of the Fire … [are] women who are dressed [but appear to be] naked." (*Muslim*, 6840)

The juxtaposed words, 'dressed naked', may indicate that although many women are dressed, their clothing is so transparent

---

*   Similar to an underskirt, slip or chemise

that it does not conceal the body underneath. Allah, exalted is He, regards them as being no different from shameless 'naked' people. And those ladies will be amongst the dwellers of the Fire.

On another occasion, the Prophet ﷺ saw a woman in a transparent dress and said:

> "She is not a woman who believes in Surat-an-Nur who wears this."
> (*Ar-Risalah*, a Maliki Manual, No: 7617)

Dressing modestly is nothing more than making a few changes to your wardrobe. If you normally wear very fitted clothes, begin to wear looser ones, which do not reveal your bodily shape. If your skirts are short, buy and wear longer ones, which do not reveal the legs. If your blouses are low cut, buy and wear ones which have small or high necks and do not reveal the bust-line and neck. If your dresses are transparent and sleeveless, buy ones which are thicker and have long sleeves. If you would rather wear trousers then ensure that you wear a long cardigan or jacket so that the buttocks and thighs are not described. Even the latest Asian fashions are becoming more and more westernised with *shalwars* (trousers) which reveal the shins, and sleeveless or see-through arms. Again, care should be taken when selecting suits or having them tailored.

In any event, whatever is worn, must not be a symbol of extravagance. The Prophet ﷺ has directed that:

> "Whoever wears a dress of fame and pride in this world, Allah will clothe him in a dress of humiliation on the Day of Rising, then set it afire."
> (*Sahih al-Bukhari*)

It is more beneficial for Muslim women to spend time pleasing Allah than pleasing the world. One may conclude this section by remembering that:

> "Allah does not look to your faces and your wealth but He looks to your heart and to your deeds." (*Muslim*)

Jerusalem : young 19th century Muslima

Lebanon : young 19th century Muslima

THE HEAD COVERING

And draw their head-coverings (*khamr*)* across their breasts. (Surat an-Nur 24: 31)

Aisha narrated that when Surat an-Nur came down:

"The women of the Ansar took the curtains, tore them and made head-covers (veils) of them." (*Sahih al-Bukhari* 6:281)

In the days of Jahiliyyah – the pre-Islamic age of ignorance – women would cover their heads but exclude their necks and chests. This was until Allah, exalted is He, revealed in the above *ayah* that the veils must be drawn over their bosoms too.

The important point to note here is that even in Pre-Islamic days it was a symbol of honour and respect for women to cover their heads. The above Qur'anic *ayah* then extended this basic requirement to incorporate the neck and bust line as this also formed part of a woman's beauty.

Is it not then embarrassing if today's women fail to adopt that which their ignorant counterparts did fifteen centuries ago?

Of course it takes a degree of courage and positive faith for a woman to adopt a symbol which due to foreign news coverage is associated with oppression.

The narrow prejudices that permeate the institutions of our society – schools, colleges and the workplace – are quick to label Muslim girls who cover their heads as oppressed or eccentric, thus making socialisation a bitter experience for them.

---

* *Khamr* is the Arabic word for cloth which covers the head and in modern days is known as the *hijab*, headscarf or traditional *dupatta*, providing it is opaque.

Ten years ago, two teenage girls from Cheshire, UK, fell victim to discrimination and were banned from wearing their *hijab*s at school for so called 'safety reasons'. But once the matter was referred to the Commission for Racial Equality the girls were allowed back into class with their scarves firmly on their heads. They stood up against all odds and those around them learnt to respect and acknowledge their achievement.

Unsurprisingly though, in order to avoid complications such as the above, most Muslim women find it easier to conform to society's norms and values rather than be the exception.

For similar reasons, some Muslim parents find it hard to encourage their daughters to cover their heads for fear of being singled out as radical and they feel the head covering will become an obstacle to a good education, career or job.

Some even go so far as to think that it would limit a woman's choice of prospective suitors. But, they forget that our destinies have already been written, as have our life partners:

"Among His Signs is that He created spouses for you of your own kind so that you might find tranquillity in them." (Surat ar-Rum 30: 21)

The question is: whom do you fear most? Your friends, family and work colleagues, or the wrath of Allah?

Clearly then, the *hijab* is not a fringe issue to be compromised. It is a direct command from Allah, the All Knowing, on which there is consensus of all Muslim schools of thought.

Just as it is compulsory to pray five times a day, so is it compulsory for Muslim women to cover their heads, necks and chests.

Fortunately, many Muslim sisters who wear the headscarf claim that it makes them feel far more liberated, as they are accepted for who they are, rather than the archetypal Barbiedolls society expects. What is more, the only thing that they attract is respect.

It has been narrated by 'Umar ibn-al-Khattab ﷺ that whilst

Photo : Peter Saunders

Turkey : Muslim women

talking on the subject of veiling with the Prophet ﷺ, he stressed three things, one of which was:

> "...I wish your wives were ordered to cover themselves from the men because good and bad ones talk to them." (*Sahih al-Bukhari* 1:395)

The Prophet ﷺ was so impressed by his views on modesty that when the *ayat* on veiling were revealed by Allah, the Prophet ﷺ relayed back to 'Umar ؓ that his wish had been endorsed.

Of course, nobody is saying that it is easy to suddenly start covering your head if it has not been the norm in your family or community. Strangely enough we often only expect our elders to cover their heads when in actual fact, the more youthful you are, the more likely that sexual advances will be made towards you which makes covering the head even more essential.

In some parts of the world, it is easier to practise wearing the headscarf as it forms part of their dress code. For example, no one ever questions the wearing of the scarf in Saudi Arabia.

But Allah, exalted is He, is:

> **"...the Lord of the two Easts and the Lord of the two Wests" (Surat ar-Rahman 55:17)**

Thus, living in the West does not exempt women from their obligations. Allah's orders must be obeyed wherever in the world one happens to live.

Thus, although the traditional wear of the women of Arabia allows them to walk comfortably around wearing a *jilbab* (outer garment), the *hijab* (headscarf) and even the *niqab* (face-mask), in the West you may prefer to wear traditional but modest Western clothes with a head covering. This would be most suitable if you are a working woman or student. Depending on your individual preference, you may prefer to wear the Asian *shalwar/kamees* with the traditional *dupatta/chaddar* around the head (though it should not be see-through).

Depending on your culture, traditions, environment and profession, what you wear can be adapted so long as the rules of Allah, exalted is He, are not.

Experience of Aisha, aged 18

"I am a student at Kings College and have been wearing the *hijab* since 6th form at school. Initially, I was quite argumentative with my parents who impressed on me the need to cover my head. This was because I felt that I would not be accepted by my peers and would not be able to keep up with the latest teenage fashions and trends. Luckily for me, the female members of my family all started wearing *hijab*, as did my best friend and I soon became more confident. I realised that my fears were triggered by my own imagination, and the whole world was not sniggering and laughing at me. To the contrary, since I started university, I have seen many proud Muslim girls in *hijab* who are respected and accepted by the non-Muslims. I have learnt that complying with Allah's orders is far greater and easier than the ever-changing values of the West."

Experience of 'Umera, aged 33

"I am a married woman with two children, aged 12 and 5, and have been working for British Airways since the age of 18.

"I first began covering my head at the later age of 31. Before this, I deliberated in fulfilling the duty for fear of what my work colleagues, who were mostly men, would say.

"Eventually when I plucked up the courage to walk into the office one morning with my head covered, the rest of the day was spent being mocked by male colleagues, which continued for many months. I recall common phrases hurled at me, such as 'terrorist', 'Scottish widow' and 'She's seen the light!' In fact, the effect was such that if the scarf happened to fall off my head, I was in no hurry to replace it.

"It was when I attended a family wedding and saw the groom's female relations all proudly wearing headscarves that the truth began to pinch. The guilt burdened me, particularly as I had made a decision not to wear the scarf that day for fear that I would look less attractive.

"I soon realised that I had to be more confident in myself and change my whole attitude towards the concept of *hijab*.

If I didn't have the courage to confront my colleagues, what would I do when I faced my Lord? It was time for me to fear Allah and not the world. This thought helped me restrengthen my iman. I sought Allah's help through *salat* (prayers), reading Islamic literature and speaking to other practising Muslim women. Eventually, after about two months, the same critical males began to respect me more and the sniggers transformed into compliments about how elegant and dignified I looked. They became more interested in Islam and I enjoyed telling them about it." Today, Umera proudly stands firm and accepts no compromises on *hijab*.

Allah, glorious is He, greatly rewarded her for her perseverance so that in April 1999 she successfully discharged the greatest duty of all, Hajj.

Experience of Anisa, aged 29

"I am a married woman with two young children, aged 8 and 5. I am a housewife and live with my in-laws.

"My decision to wear the *hijab* came about after I accomplished my first 'umrah (shorter pilgrimage) in 1992. Having just visited the House of Allah, I felt as though I had been granted a new lease of life and was eager to be more modest in my conduct upon my return to England. Wearing the *hijab* makes me feel closer to Allah, exalted is He. It acts as a constant protection against all evil.

"I was also amongst the first women to set a trend at my children's school encouraging mothers to cover their heads.

"Where we once used to be more concerned about gossiping and the latest fashions and films, now most of the Muslim women enjoy conversing about Islamic issues and the number of women practising *hijab* is on the increase." Anisa too, completed her Hajj this year.

Experience of Maria, aged 27

"I am a qualified barrister and a practising Muslim. My religious beliefs were cemented whilst I was an undergraduate at university. By regularly attending Islamic circles, debates and conferences I had no difficulty in adopting the scarf as all my peers were doing the same. We were like a close knit family and all had the same spiritual aim.

"Surprisingly, I faced problems, not in public but in private.

My own father was my greatest hurdle. He labelled me as a 'fundamentalist' and I found myself constantly arguing with him. He had convinced himself that I would never be able to find a suitable partner and eventually I was forced to stop wearing the scarf.

"One day I read the following explanatory note on Surah Luqman which provided me with a solution to the problem:

"'Where the duty to man conflicts with the duty to Allah, it means that there is something wrong with the human will and we should obey Allah rather than man. But do not be arrogant or insolent in your reasoning.' (From the commentary in *The Noble Qur'an* on Surah Luqman: 15 by Yusuf Ali)

"When I read this, I realised that I must obey Allah and my duty was to gently persuade my father to see sense without seeming to be rebellious and ruthless. Eventually with Allah's help I succeeded and resumed wearing the scarf."

Maria is now happily married. Incidentally, she received her marriage proposal whilst in *hijab*.

From all the interviews carried out with the above ladies, it is clear that the right-acting go through a prolonged test of fire. Patience, truthfulness and iman in Allah must be tried and it is only through this process that women can develop real strength and courage.

After reading the above, it may seem that sometimes Islam requires us to do something we do not like, but as stated in the Qur'an:

"It may be that you hate something when it is good for you and it may be that you love something when it is bad for you. Allah knows and you do not know." (Surat al-Baqarah 2: 216)

Your *Mahram*

They should only display their adornments to their husbands or their fathers or their husbands' fathers, or their sons or their husbands' sons or their brothers or their brothers' sons or their sisters' sons or other women or those they own as slaves or their male attendants who have no sexual desire or children who still have no awareness of women's private parts.... **(Surat an-Nur: 31)**

The word *mahram* denotes a relationship either by marriage, or by close blood ties of such a degree that marriage is permanently prohibited. Thus, for a woman a *mahram* is any of the above which can, for the sake of simplicity, be listed as follows:

a. Husbands
b. Fathers
c. Grandfathers
d. Sons
e. Stepsons
f. Brothers
g. Nephews

Any man who falls outside the ambit of the list such as 'male cousins' and 'in-laws' will be classed as a non-*mahram* and Islam prohibits a lady and a non-*mahram* male being alone together. The slaves and male attendants mentioned in the *ayah* are permitted to be in the more intimate circumstances of the family, but are not *mahram* as such.

Islam does not permit the free mixing of men and women outside the close family group. The following Qur'anic *ayah* of Surat al-Ahzab defined this:

"...When you ask his wives for something, ask them from behind a screen. That is purer for your hearts and their hearts." (Surat al-Ahzab 33: 53)

It is clear from the time of the Prophet ﷺ that the companions did not regard the above *ayah* as referring exclusively to the Prophet's wives but by implication to all women.

Undoubtedly, the wives of the Prophet ﷺ were true role models and regarded as 'Mothers of the Muminin'. If they could only be addressed from behind a screen to avoid any impropriety, how crucial it must then be for ordinary women, who compared to the Prophet's wives are a greater source of temptation, to avoid freely socialising with men.

The importance of the above was emphasised by eminent poet, philosopher and religious scholar, Muhammad Iqbal, who said:

"Our women's veiled segregation is not due to the fact that men are immoral. A woman in fact, is the Lord's holiest creature. And her sex relationship necessitates that she must live immune from undesirable eyes... In this world, woman is the most sacred means of procreation and it is a fact that creative functionaries lie always hidden and concealed in life." (*Iqbal in Quotes* p.64, 65)

On the relationship of the 'in-law', the Prophet ﷺ said:

"The in-law is death." (*Sahih al-Bukhari*)

The reasoning behind this is not that there is a lack of trust in either of them but rather that such caution protects them from wrong thoughts, sexual feelings and the potential immorality that can arise naturally. Indeed, as a result of a liaison between women and in-laws, jealousy, suspicion and hostility may arise and many marriages may be ruined. Thus Allah, exalted is He, wanted to avoid the severing of family ties in this bitter and uncivil way.

The Prophet ﷺ has also said:

"Whoever believes in Allah and the Last Day must never be in seclusion with a woman without there being a *mahram* of hers, for otherwise, shaytan will be the third person (with them)." (*Sahih al-Bukhari*)[37]

These days, attending mixed schools and colleges, going to work in a mixed and 'multi-cultural' society make it difficult to always have a *mahram* present with you which means that women can be a greater source of temptation. Intermingling to some extent is inevitable, but must be limited to what is absolutely and the individual is always the best judge of his/her own conduct.

In the United Arab Emirates, the need for having separate centres for women has been considered and a 'She Zone' (women-only mall) is due to open in Abu Dhabi which would hold forty-two air-conditioned shops and cinemas. Clearly, this would assist the free movement and expression of women in the east. However, the likelihood of having such places in the western world is remote. For this reason, women need to be more cautious about how they interact with non-*mahram*s.

It has been narrated that the Messenger of Allah ﷺ said:

"It is better for one of you to be pricked in the head with an iron pick than to touch a woman whom it is unlawful to touch." (Narrated by Ma'qal ibn Yasar reported by al-Tabarani)

Thus, talking to male colleagues at work or college to seek some advice and share opinions, or interviewing your client or patient who happens to be male can be pardoned, but outward free-mixing and flirtatiousness such as socialising at parties, staying behind at school or college to engage in idle talk is extremely disapproved.

According to a hadith:

"A woman who freely mixes with other people and shows off her decoration is without light and virtue." (*Sahih al-Bukhari*)

Bosnia: Muslim women

NOT TO STAMP YOUR FEET

Nor should they stamp their feet so that their hidden ornaments are known... (Surat an-Nur 24: 31)

The underlying theme of the above is that women should avoid the kind of behaviour, which draws the attention of men. Similarly they should avoid:

a) Toying with their ornaments

b) Speaking in a soft alluring way

c) Use of perfume and excessive use of cosmetics.

Pre-Islamic women used to stamp their feet when they passed by men so that the jingling of their ankle bracelets might be heard. This was one of the tricks of showy women, which the Qur'an forbids.

It is not difficult to understand the reason for the above prohibition. Obviously, the woman who decks herself out, walks seductively, toys with her jewellery, persistently flicks her hair, talks invitingly and wears too much make-up, will always attract men.

As stated in the Noble Qur'an, a woman must walk and talk in a dignified manner avoiding flirtatiousness in her facial expressions and movements:

"Do not be too soft-spoken in your speech lest someone with sickness in his heart becomes desirous." (Surat al-Ahzab 33: 32)

If it is recognised that women are by nature caring and shy, their gentility would naturally be reflected in their speech.

Women must not forget that the 'voice' is also a form of attraction and the softer and sweeter one speaks to non-*mahram* males, the greater the likelihood of attraction. The reason for the above injunction then, is not because of the fear of women's misbehaviour or mistrust of them, but the danger to them from opportunistic men. This does not mean that women should be rude or insulting but rather their tone of voice must be direct and business-like so that men are not encouraged.

Similarly, there is the Islamic ruling concerning the use of perfumes, as here again, a man's desires can be aroused. Even the classic 'impulse' adverts serve to remind us of the effects of alluring fragrances. It has been narrated that:

> "The woman who perfumes herself and passes through a gathering is an adulteress and any eye which is attracted to her is that of an adulterer."
> (*Abu Dawud, at-Tirmidhi, an-Nasa'i, Ibn Khuzaymah* and *Ibn Hibban*)

Allah, exalted is He, does not wish women to make a vulgar worldly display of themselves as in the Jahiliyyah where women dressed extravagantly and wore cosmetics in excess. This is stressed in Surat al-Ahzab:

> **"...and do not display your beauty as it was previously displayed in the Time of Ignorance." (Surat al-Ahzab 33: 33)**

However, this does not preclude Muslim women from beautifying or perfuming themselves to please their husbands.

Conclusion

As Muslims, we have a duty to help one another in right action and duty (Surat al-Ma'idah 5: 2)* and I have written this short book with this aim in mind.

One of the greatest problems of our society is the lack of knowledge of the deen. The Prophet Muhammad ﷺ said:

> "Seeking knowledge is obligatory for every Muslim." (*Sahih al-Bukhari*)

When people of knowledge exist in the Muslim community whom one can ask for knowledge and Islamic literature is translated into almost every language, there is no excuse for neglecting this duty. Even the Greek philosopher Socrates said, "Vice is the result of ignorance and virtue is power." All Muslim men and women then need to strengthen their roots in the Islamic tradition by not only by learning from the people of knowledge and reading and learning more but also understanding and imparting more.

I hope that after reading this, my Muslim sisters will look again at their individual lives and, if necessary, revise their conduct in accordance with the Qur'an and Sunnah. If conduct is in need of change, then change will be gradual. This requires patience, perseverance and above all, self-criticism and accountability. Once faults are identified, correcting them becomes easier.

I pray that Allah, the Most Beneficent, and the Most Merciful, forgives us our past wrong actions and guides us all in our future

---

* "Help each other to goodness and taqwa. Do not help each other to wrong-doing and enmity."

spiritual endeavours. May He help the Muslim women of the world to be modest in their manners and virtuous at all times and as He has promised:

For those who have *taqwa* there is triumph: Gardens…

(Surat an-Naba 78: 31-32)

TEST YOUR KNOWLEDGE

1. In which Qur'anic Surah will you find the basic commands on correct Islamic conduct for men and women and what are the five basic commands?

2. Which command on modesty is applicable to both men and women?

3. What is the meaning of the word *zina*?

4. What is the Prophet Muhammad's guidance ﷺ on the first and second look?

5. In accordance with Islamic shari'ah, what constitutes beauty and ornaments?

6. What are the three basic requirements of modesty in dress?

7. What is meant by 'dressed but naked'?

8. What does the Qur'an say about the rules on dress for elderly women?

9. What is the meaning of the word 'jahiliyyah'?

10. What is the *hijab* and its purpose?

11. Who is not your *mahram*?

12. When is *khalwah* permitted between men and women?

13. What does the Prophet Muhammad ﷺ say on the relationship of in-laws?

14. What must women not do to draw attention to their hidden ornaments?

15. What did the Prophet Muhammad ﷺ consider to be one of the most precious things in the world?

The Noble Woman

Muslim sisters, hear my call
    Raise your status, stand up tall,
Lower your gaze and safe you'll be
    From every step to adultery.

Don't display and flaunt your beauty
    Wear *hijab*, fulfil your duty.
Draw your veils before those Allah said;
    Protect your charms for the man you wed.

Conduct yourself in a dignified way
    And avoid making a dazzling display
Do not walk seductively
    Do not talk invitingly.

Shaytan will try to make you sin
    Refrain from evil, don't let him win.
The only way you can get to heaven
    Is by striving to be a Noble Woman.